First
Christmas

Investigation of the Evidence

Ralph O. Muncaster

Published by:

Mission Viejo, California 92691

Scripture quotations taken from the HOLY BIBLE, NEW INTERNATIONAL VERSION. Copyright © 1973, 1978, 1984 by International Bible Society. Used by permission of Zondervan Publishing House.

First
Christmas

Investigation of the Evidence

By Ralph O. Muncaster

Published by:

Mission Viejo, CA 92691 U.S.A.

\All rights reserved. No part of this book may be reproduced or transmitted in any form or by any means, electronic or mechanical, including photocopying, recording or by any information storage and retrieval system without written permission from the author, except for the inclusion of brief quotations in a review.

Copyright © 1996 by Ralph O. Muncaster
First Printing 1995
Second Printing 1996, completely revised
Printed in the United States of America

ISBN 1-888904-02-X

First Christmas
Investigation of the Evidence

First Christmas - *The Real Issues* 5
The World at Jesus' Birth 6
Christmas - The Historical Record 7
The Christmas Witnesses 8
Manuscript Evidence of Jesus' Birth 9
Non-Christian Evidence 10
Archaeological Evidence 11
Christmas Prophecy - "Proof" 12
The First Christmas - Key Historical Issues ... 14
Ancestors of Jesus - *Before David* 16
                     - *After David* 17
The Journey to Bethlehem 18
The Night of Jesus' Birth 20
The Magi 21
When Was Jesus Born? 22
Was Jesus Just a Man? 23
Was Jesus God? 24
Common Questions 25
References 27

First Christmas - *The Biblical Account*

Luke 1, 2 & 3	❏ Zechariah, Elizabeth & John the Baptist ❏ Mary, Joseph... appearance of angels ❏ Birth of Jesus, shepherds ❏ Jesus' circumcision, Simeon and Anna ❏ Mary's genealogy [Luke 3]
Matthew 1 & 2	❏ Joseph's genealogy ❏ Angel's appearance to Joseph ❏ The Magi ❏ Escape to Egypt & return to Nazareth

The First Christmas
What If... ?

What if the *Biblical* account of the First Christmas is all true?

Then it's certainly a message of great joy for all who accept God's plan... for all who establish a relationship with him.

The message of Christmas goes beyond the birth of an infant, beyond shepherds, a star, Bethlehem and the Magi. The basic message of Christmas deals with an age old promise. A promise of God in human flesh... A promise of an eternal Savior. The first Christmas is just the prelude to the in-depth description of how to have a relationship with God, forever. A relationship that promises an eternity of no more tears, no more death, no more pain and unbelievable joy. The alternative, however, is a horror beyond description. Christmas involves both sides... A promise of good, and a promise of bad. And it provides a clear way for everyone to choose the promise of good.

So if the *Biblical* account of Christmas is true, it means everyone must choose his own destiny... today and eternally. This makes the truth of Christmas, without a doubt, the most important issue for anyone to understand in one's lifetime... More important than the next vacation, more important than the next golf game, and even more important than the next paycheck.

Fortunately God has provided more evidence of the Christmas message than in any event in human history. We don't need to accept it on blind faith alone. Even so, like acceptance of any historical fact or religious belief, the ultimate decision to believe and to follow requires a final step of faith.

First Christmas - *The Real Issues*

The baby born the First Christmas... Jesus Christ... has been analyzed FAR more than anyone in the history of the world.

Did Jesus Really Exist?

1.

The existence of Jesus is one of the best established facts in history. Thousands of early manuscripts surviving major eradication attempts, provides greater support than for any other accepted historical fact. And the confirmation of early Christian Martyrs... alive at the time of Jesus... is undeniable.
[pp 7-13]

2.

Was Jesus just a man?

Just a great prophet?

Just a great teacher?

Evidence suggests otherwise. Miracles of Jesus were widely acknowledged... even by non-Believers. Century old prophecies provide "proof" of God's intervention. Even indirect archaeological evidence exists regarding the Resurrection. But the disciples who knew the truth... willingly, even joyfully, gave their lives to confirm what they knew. Compelling evidence.
[pp 16-17, 22-24]

Who Was Jesus?

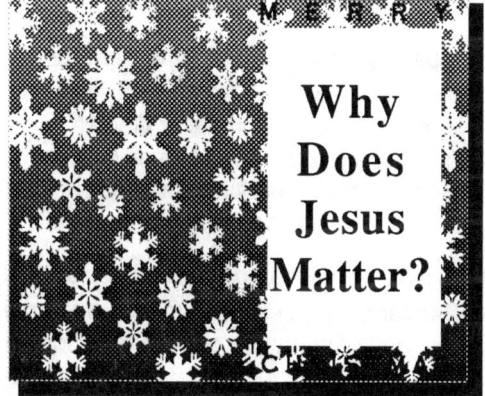

Why Does Jesus Matter?

3.

Joy on earth and forever.

Strength to face any challenge.

Eternal life with God.

Everyone must make a choice to accept or reject the baby born on the First Christmas. No decision is also a choice... of rejection. Jesus offers the above free gifts to anyone.
[pp 22-26]

The World at Jesus' Birth

The stage was perfectly set for the First Christmas.

The World Situation

Political Stability - Never before or since has such a large percentage of the world lived at peace under a single government. The Roman Empire had expanded to include much of Europe, Africa and Asia. About half of the world's 138 million people were governed by Rome. And the peace known as *Pax Romana*, admired throughout history, lasted 200 years.

In 44 BC Julius Caesar was assassinated and had bequeathed his throne to his great grand nephew, Octavian, who was given the title Caesar Augustus. After defeating Mark Anthony and Cleopatra, Augustus ruled from 27 BC to 14 AD. Augustus began the great peace reforms and ordered a worldwide census [Luke 2:1] which historians believe may have been the census that brought Mary and Joseph to Bethlehem. (See page 21 - *When Was Jesus Born?*)

Transportation - For the first time in history an elaborate network of highways and sea routes made transportation throughout the empire relatively easy. This was vital to the rapid spread of Christianity.

Communication - The world was becoming unified as the level of education increased, and the language of Koine Greek was becoming common (the dialect of the *New Testament*). As a result, it was easier and quicker to spread new ideas and thinking across a multi-cultural world than ever before.

Bethlehem, Nazareth & Jerusalem

Jerusalem was the most prominent city in the Middle East. Along with being the political and religious center for the Jewish people, it was a regional seat of government of Rome and the residence of Herod.

Nazareth was on a major trade route from the ports of Tyre and Sidon, both known for vice and prostitution... as was Nazareth. The great city of Sepphoris, just 4 miles from Nazareth, was the capital of Galilee in Jesus' youth and was being rapidly expanded to honor its new leader, Herod Antipas. As carpenters, Joseph and Jesus almost certainly spent time there. (Excavation of Sepphoris is far from complete.)

Bethlehem of Judea was a small rural town, located a few miles south of Jerusalem. Even in Jesus' day, Bethlehem had significance as the burial place of Rachel (Jacob's wife), the place of courtship of Ruth and Boaz, and the birthplace of King David.

Christmas - The Historical Record

The historical record regarding the **birth** of most great people is very limited. Consider John F. Kennedy or Julius Caesar... how much do we know about either's birth? Relatively speaking, we know a lot about the First Christmas. Primary sources are *Luke* and *Matthew* within the *Bible*.

Luke - Credibility of Luke as a historian was verified by none other than (perhaps) the world's greatest archaeologist, Sir William Ramsay, a skeptic who began extensive research to disprove Luke. His colleagues expected Ramsay to uncover evidence to disprove much of the *New Testament* once and for all. Yet Ramsay's final analysis surprised nearly everyone. After thirty years of study, Ramsay found Luke to be accurate in every detail. Ramsay even labeled Luke as one of the "...greatest historians of all time". Not surprisingly, Ramsay converted to Christianity.

How Evidence was Collected

Like any biography, evidence was conducted through interviews with people and study of records at the time [Luke 1:1-4]. The importance of Luke's work, *during the time of the eyewitnesses*, is often overlooked.

Luke's (and Matthew's) information was collected and recorded during the lifetime of those involved. Any time history is documented in the lifetime of contemporaries, *it must stand the test of eyewitness critics*. Otherwise it would not be accepted and would vanish into obscurity. Today, if someone wrote that John F. Kennedy was born from a virgin and rose from the dead, it would NOT become a widely accepted historical record.

The events of Jesus were quite remarkable and certainly would have been corroborated at length. If there was not exceptional eyewitness agreement about the events... including the virgin birth, the miracles and the resurrection... undoubtedly the historical record would have quickly vanished. Instead it became, by far, the most recorded account ever.

"People Talked"

Founders of other religions claim divine insight from *solitary moments* with angels or gods - an easy claim to fabricate. In contrast, the *Bible* indicates many people discussed the extraordinary events:

Zechariah... Loss & regaining of sight - [Luke 1:21-22; Luke 1:65-66]
Elizabeth... Miracle child - [Luke 1:57-58]
Shepherds... Regarding angels and birth of Jesus - [Luke 2:17-18]
Herod... Regarding the birth of Jesus - [Matt. 2:16]
500 People... The Resurrection of Jesus - [1 Cor. 15:6-7]

Hundreds of people witnessed these events, not just a few fanatics.

The Christmas Witnesses

Consider again, John F. Kennedy or Julius Caesar or any such historical figure. Why do we have so little eyewitness testimony about their births? Perhaps because nothing really startling happened. Jesus' birth was different. The events were <u>memorable</u>. And there were many witnesses so events could easily be verified later during Luke's investigation.

Consider the shepherds [Lk 2:17-18]. What would prompt low-status shepherds to widely proclaim the "amazing events"? Others probably thought a miraculous appearance of angels, followed by the prophetic discovery of Jesus, was strange or untrue. Bethlehem was a small town. When Luke wrote about it later, events could easily be corroborated by eyewitnesses.

Consider Simeon and Anna [Lk 2:25-38]. These were two well known, highly esteemed people. Both proclaimed the infant Jesus to be the long awaited Messiah... a powerful statement to be made by such respected individuals. Perhaps at the time the proclamations were simply acknowledged. Later they became highly significant. Again, others were eyewitnesses to these statements.

Consider Zechariah and Elizabeth [Lk 1:21-58]. It would have been a very serious offense for Zechariah to falsify events concerning a vision of angels during holy ceremonies, or to give false prophecy. Yet Zechariah indicated to other priests that his barren wife, Elizabeth, would bear a son. With no ultrasound in those days and given that Elizabeth was well past childbearing age, such statements would have been very costly if untrue. And the loss and return of Zechariah's speech as foretold by the angels, added weight to the prophecy. Again, eyewitnesses were present who would have recalled such events.

> **Other Unforgettable Events**
>
> Herod's slaughter of innocent children would not have been forgotten by local people recounting the events of the First Christmas. Even the visit by the Magi would have been unforgettable. The Magi were powerful men who would have arrived with a lot of fanfare [p 20].

Consider finally, witnesses to statements of deity proclaimed at Jesus' birth - later verified by his death and resurrection. His deity was proclaimed <u>*before birth*</u> by angels, by Elizabeth and Zechariah [Lk 1:43] and by Mary. It was proclaimed <u>*at birth*</u> by angels... witnessed by shepherds. And it was proclaimed <u>*soon after birth*</u> by Simeon and Anna. His deity was foretold in scores of prophecies and was later confirmed by resurrection from death... seen by hundreds of witnesses [1 Cor 15:6].

Manuscript Evidence of Jesus' Birth

Although evidence shows that Luke's original history would be accurately recorded in the face of eyewitnesses... how do we know the account was not changed over time? The answer is in the explosion of recorded copies of evidence *within a very short time of the actual events*. Today, we have in existence, *many more early manuscripts about Jesus than for any other event up to that period... Even events widely accepted as fact.*

Comparison to Historical Manuscripts[9]

Julius Caesar's great campaigns in France have been taught as historical fact for centuries. The detailed history relies on Caesar's recording of the "*Gallic Wars*" written in the first century BC. How does such a prominent history compare in evidence to the accounts of the First Christmas? *It's not even in the same league.* In fact no other event of antiquity even comes close to the documentary evidence of the life of Jesus. We have in existence today, over 24,000 early manuscripts of the *New Testament* compared to only 10 of the Gallic Wars. Copies exist that were written within 25 years of Jesus - versus 1000 years for the earliest *Gallic Wars*.

Ancient Work Title	Existing Early Manuscripts	Elapsed Time: Event to Earliest Manuscript
Gallic Wars (History)	10	1,000 years
Pliny the Younger (History)	7	750 years
Thucydides (History)	8	1,300 years
Herodotus (History)	8	1,300 years
Sophocles	193	1,400 years
Euripides	9	1,500 years
Aristotle	49	1,400 years
Aristophanes	10	1,200 years
New Testament	24,000+	25 years

Attempts to Eradicate Evidence

The existing early documentation of the *New Testament* would be incredible enough if times were "normal" then. However, in the first three centuries a number of opponents attempted to eradicate the *New Testament* and Christianity. Why? Because it was a threat to many peoples' livelihood. Religious leaders and many merchants had to choose. Sale of idols plummeted causing some to request execution [p 10].

Of course some early Jews attempted to stop the spread of Christianity through persecution. Nero and Rome increased persecution substantially. In 303 AD an edict was issued to destroy all *Bibles*. Anyone caught with a *Bible* was condemned to death.

Non-Christian Evidence

Very few written works *of anything* exist from the period of 30 to 60 AD. All works from the 50's and 60's AD are said to fit in bookends only a foot apart[9]. Nero's killing of Christians in 64 AD led to some writing.

Thallus [c. AD 52] - Historical work referenced by Julius Africanus - Explains the darkness at the time of Christ's death as a solar eclipse. While an eclipse did not occur in that period (pointed out by Julius Africanus), reference to Jesus' death was stated as a matter-of-fact.

Josephus [c. AD 64 - 93] - This Jewish historian referenced Jesus, his miracles, his crucifixion and his disciples. Also referenced are James... "brother of Jesus who was called the Christ" and John the Baptist.

Cornelius Tacitus [AD 64 - 116] - Writing to dispel rumors that Nero caused the great fire of Rome in 64 AD, he refers to Christians as the followers of "Christus", who "had undergone the death penalty in the reign of Tiberius, by sentence of the procurator Pontius Pilatus." The Resurrection was called "the pernicious superstition."

Pliny the Younger [c. AD 112] - As governor of Bithynia (Asia Minor) he requested guidance from Rome regarding the proper test to give Christians before executing them. (If they renounced the faith, cursed Jesus and worshiped the statue of emperor Trajan, they were set free).

Hadrian [c. AD 117 - 138] - In response to questions regarding the punishment of Christians who drew people away from pagan gods which affected the sale of idols, Hadrian said that they be "examined" regarding their faith (similar to the response to Pliny the Younger).

Suetonius [c. AD 120] - A historian wrote about events in the late 40's - 60's AD that identify Christ, the "mischievous and novel superstition" of the Resurrection, and of Christians being put to death by Nero.

Phlegon [c. AD 140] - Referenced by Julius Africanus and Origen - referred to "eclipse", earthquake and Jesus' prophecies.

Lucian of Samosata [c. AD 170] - Greek satirist Lucian wrote about Christians, Christ, the crucifixion, Christian martyrs and "novel beliefs."

Mara Bar-Serapion [c. AD 70+] - A Syrian philosopher wrote from prison to his son comparing Jesus to Socrates and Plato.

Writings from Jewish Rabbis

Several passages from the *Talmud* and other Jewish writings clearly refer to Jesus Christ.

- "Hanging" (on a cross) of Jesus on the eve of Passover [written: circa AD 40 - 180] .
- Identifying Jesus and the names of 5 disciples.
- Healing in the name of Jesus.
- Scoffing at the "claim" of a virgin birth, and implying "illegitimacy."

Archaeological Evidence

Archaeologists have discovered substantial support about many details of Jesus' life (*Bible - Archaeological Facts*, p 28). Some examples include:

Jesus' Birthplace[11]

To us, a "stable" is a type of wooden barn outside a home. In Jesus' day, stables were often within courtyards of homes or in caves outside. The actual site believed to be the "stable" of Jesus birth was identified relatively shortly after his Resurrection. Early authors (Jerome and Paulinus of Nola) indicate it was "marked" about the time of Hadrian (c. 120 AD). Archaeologists have never seriously disputed it. The site is a cave located beneath the *Church of the Nativity* in Bethlehem.

Indirect Resurrection Evidence[4]

Evidence that the people in Jesus' time believed in the Resurrection is found on bone caskets (ossuaries) discovered in a sealed tomb outside Jerusalem in 1945. Coins minted in about 50 AD were found inside the caskets, dating the burial within about 20 years of Jesus' crucifixion. Markings are clearly legible including the words (in Greek): "Jesus, Help" and "Jesus, Let Him Arise". The caskets also contain several crosses, clearly marked in charcoal. This is powerful evidence that early Christians believed in Jesus' ability to triumph over death.

Prior to the Resurrection, "grave robbing" was not considered a serious offense. The Resurrection changed that. An inscription found on a tomb in Nazareth warns that anyone found stealing from the tombs would receive the death penalty. Scholars believe the inscription was written as early as Tiberius (c. 37 BC) or as late as Claudius (41-54 AD). In either case, it would have been shortly after the crucifixion. Naturally Jesus' hometown of Nazareth would be an obvious city of "interest" to officials.

Jesus Burial Shroud?

A burial shroud (*Shroud of Turin*) is considered by many to be the actual burial shroud of Jesus [Mt 27:59, Mk 15:46, Lk 23:53]. Several items support authenticity:

1. Tests that confirm fiber type and small particles of limestone dust unique to the region.
2. Confirmation of blood, in wounds precisely as indicated in the accounts of Jesus' unique execution.
3. Confirmation of a crucifixion as a likely cause of the type of image created... matching a deceased body.
4. Coins on eyes dated about the time of crucifixion.

Some experts have been able to mimic creation of the shroud's image using today's technology. Some believe it to be a complex fourteenth century hoax. The ultimate issue of it's use for Jesus, however, will never be certain.

Christmas Prophecy - "Proof"

Although history can never be "proven", enormous statistical probability is often viewed as "proof" by scientists and mathematicians. From a statistical viewpoint, God's involvement in the life of Jesus is "certain".

As indicated earlier, the prophecies contained in the *Old Testament* were written long before Jesus. The *Dead Sea Scrolls* provide irrefutable evidence that they were not tampered with over the centuries. Of the 469 prophecies contained in the *Old Testament* that would have been fulfilled, 467 have been verified (we have no record of fulfillment of two). Perhaps the most fascinating prophecies are those about Jesus.

Who

Ancestors in Prophesy:

David	[2 Samuel 7:12-16, Jer 23:5]
Jesse	[Isaiah 11]
Judah	[Isaiah 11]
Jacob	[Gen 35:10-12, Num 24:17]
Isaac	[Genesis 17:16, 21:12]
Abraham	[Genesis 12:3, 22:18]
Shem	[Genesis 9:26-27; 10]

What

Virgin Birth	[Isaiah 7:14]
Birth of Eternal Savior	[Isaiah 9:6-7]
Savior to Jews and Gentiles	[Isaiah 49:6]
Miracle Worker	[Isaiah 29:18, 35:5-6]
Rejection by Jews	[Is 53:1-3, Ps 118:22]
	[Matt 21:42-46]

When

Prophecy of the Date of Palm Sunday

[Daniel 9:20-27] Although complex until understood, this prophecy made about 535 BC, *predicted Jesus' final entry into Jerusalem <u>to the day</u>*. The prophecy states:

> **Daniel's "Seventy Sevens"**

- 69 periods of 7 (years) will pass from the decree to rebuild Jerusalem until the coming of the "Anointed One" (Messiah, in Hebrew). This dates Jesus' entry into Jerusalem on Palm Sunday.

- After that time the Anointed One will be cut off (Hebrew: "yikaret", meaning a sudden, violent end... crucifixion).

- And after that time the city and the temple will be destroyed.

Prophecy: Daniel, a Hebrew, received the prophetic revelation in 535 BC. Using the *Hebrew* definition of year (360 days) we find:

69 times 7 years = 173,880 days.

The actual decree to rebuild Jerusalem was given by Artaxerxes[1] on March 14, 445 BC (First day of Nisan that year - Nehemiah 2:1-6).

Using the *actual* 365 day calendar along with adjustments for leap years, and the final scientific adjustment (leap year dropped every 128 years), we find this number of days brings us precisely to[19]:

> April 6, 32 AD

History: Jesus' ministry began in the *15th year* of Tiberius Caesar [Luke 3:1], whose reign began in 14 AD. A chronological analysis of Jesus' ministry shows 3 years leading up to the final week, in 32 AD.

The Royal Observatory in Greenwich, England Confirms the Sunday before Passover that year to be...

> April 6, 32 AD

Other prophecy elements were fulfilled as well:

- Jesus was crucified three and a half days later.
- The Romans destroyed the city and temple in 70 AD.

Where

Precise City of Jesus' Birth

The *Bible* [Micah 5:2] specified that Jesus would be born in Bethlehem, in Ephrathah (i.e. Judea... there was another Bethlehem closer to Joseph's home in Nazareth).

Other Prophecies

- ❑ King on a donkey [Zech 9:9]
- ❑ Crucified, pierced [Ps 22:16]
- ❑ No bones broken [Ps 22:17]
- ❑ Pierced with a spear [Zech 12:10]
- ❑ Betrayal by friend [Ps 41:9]
- ❑ Suffering, rejected [Is 53:1-3]
- ❑ Cast lots for clothing [Ps 22:18]
- ❑ Given gall & wine [Ps 69:20-22]
- ❑ Posterity to serve him [Ps 22:30]
- ❑ For 30 pieces silver [Zech 11:12]
- ❑ ...Silver cast on temple floor ...Used to buy potter's field [Zech 11:13]

Statistics experts estimate the probability of all prophecies coming true in ANY one man is about one chance in 10^{99}... less than the odds of correctly selecting one electron out of all the matter in the universe... or essentially zero *without divine intervention.*[9]

The First Christmas

1. The Prophecies

Detailed prophecies foretold many facts about the Messiah [pp 12-13]:

Who he would be,
What he would do,
When he would come,
Where He would be born.

2. The Star

A bright star appeared t[hat] triggered the visit of Ma[gi] from the east [p 25].

12. Archaeology

Archaeologists believe they have located the site of Jesus' birth. Other compelling evidence of existence of Jesus, and the wide circulation of the Resurrection and it's impact on people has been discovered [p 11].

11. The Jewish Record

Even those violently opposed to Jesus provide historical evidence including indisputable prophecy and references in writings such as the *Talmud* [p 10].

10. The Disciple's Martyrdom

Eleven people who *certainly knew the truth* of Jesus and the Resurrection, willingly - even joyfully died to support the historical account. This was not some impulsive slaughter, but a purposeful effort of disciples to ensure the historical record remained intact, in spite of the cost of eventual execution [p 23].

9. Historical Martyrs

Millions of people, many able to communicate with eyewitnesses willingly died to preserve the historical record [p 22].

Key Historical Issues

3. The Christmas Witnesses

Many people saw the unusual events of the first Christmas and corroborated the account widely circulated at the time. Only an accurate record could have survived such scrutiny [p 8].

4. Herod's Slaughter

An insecure tyrant, Herod commanded slaughter of all children under 2 years old in the area. Estimates suggest about sixty children were murdered. [p 20]

5. The Magi

Powerful visitors came from the east. They knew about the coming Messiah from the teaching of Daniel, who was leader of the Magi during the Exile. Herod was compelled to meet these important visitors (the subject of many myths) [p 20].

6. Paul's Change

A prominent leader of the persecution of Christians gave up wealth position and status once he encountered the risen Jesus. Paul recorded most of the New Testament [p 23].

7. Rapid Church Formation

Events caused the formation of the church - a body that survived the most focused and intensive persecution of all time [p 9].

t Explosion

or since has olosion of event ever ith the birth, f Jesus. The cord was ny thousands sses [p 9].

Ancestors of Jesus - Before David

Genealogies were especially important to the Hebrews. Ancestors played a vital role in many legal rights. Only men (fathers) were included in official genealogies since few rights were given to women. Examination of the ancestors of Jesus provides many insights. In fact, Jesus descended from a wide variety of people including a prostitute, murderers, adulterers blastphemers and even children born from incest. This should give everyone hope regardless of ancestral background.

From Adam to Noah to Abraham [Gen 5]

At least one scholar has determined the genealogy from Adam to Noah contains a veiled prophecy of a Savior to come. The root meanings of names are:

Man - Appointed - Mortal - Sorrow - The Blessed God - Shall come down - Teaching - His Death shall bring - The despairing - Comfort[13].

Adam	(Man)	Jared	(Shall come down)
Seth	(Appointed)	Enoch	(Teaching)
Enosh	(Mortal)	Methuselah	(His death will bring)
Kenan	(Sorrow)	Lamech	(The despairing)
Mahalalel	(The Blessed God)	Noah	(Comfort)

Abraham was a pivotal person in history. He was considered both the father of the Jews (Isaac - *Old Testament*) and of the Arabs (Ishmael - *OT* and *Qur'an*).

Shem to Abraham (*Luke*)

Gen 5:32; 10:21	Shem
Gen 10:22; 11:10	Arphaxad
Gen 10:24	Salah
Gen 10:24	Ever
Gen 11:18	Peleg
Gen 11:18	Rue
Gen 11:20	Serug
Gen 11:22	Nahor
Gen 11:24	Terah
Gen 11:27; 17:5	Abraham

Luke, a doctor, provides the natural genealogy of Jesus from Adam to Mary.

Matthew, a tax collector writing primarily to the Jews, starts with Abraham and provides the official "legal" line through the "husband of Mary" - Joseph.

Isaac to David (*Luke* and *Matthew*)

Gen 17:19; 21:3	Isaac
Gen 25:26; 27:36	Jacob ("Israel")
Gen 29:35; 46:12	Judah
Gen 38:29; Ruth 4:12	Pharez
Gen 46:; Ruth 4:18	Hezron
Ruth 4:19; 1 Chron 2:9	Ram
Num 1:7; 2:3; Ruth 4:19	Amminadab
Num 1:7; 2:3; Ruth 4:20	Nahshon
Ruth 4:20; 1 Chron 2:11	Salmon
Ruth 2:1; 4:21; Mt 1:5	Boaz (wife: Ruth)
Ruth 4:17; 21	Obed
Ruth 4:17; 21; 1 Sam 16:1	Jesse
Ruth 4:17; 22; 1 Sam 16:13	David

Tamar - Tricked her father-In-Law Judah into thinking she was a prostitute (hiding behind a veil) to enable their sexual relations to produce a child and heir. Tamar produced twins, Pharez (Perez) became ancestor of Christ. [Gen 38:1-30].

Ruth - Gentile bride of Boaz. Becomes a prophetic model of the Church, with Boaz a "type" of Christ - or Redeemer[14].

Pharez to David - Jewish law required 10 generations before any heir born through incest could have certain rights - including becoming king [Deut 23:2]. This is why Saul became the first King of Israel even though prophecy had already indicated the king would come from Jesse & Judah [Is 11].

Ancestors of Jesus - *After David*

After David, Mary's line went through David's son Nathan, Joseph went through David's son Solomon:

David

	Mary's line		Joseph's line
2 Sam 5:14	Nathan	2 Sam 12:24-25;	Solomon
Lk 3:31	Mattatha	1 Ch 3:5; 14:4; 23:1;	
Lk 3:31	Menan	2 Ch 1:12; 1 Ki 11:1	
Lk 3:31	Melea	1 Ki 11:43;14:21;	Rehoboam
Lk 3:30	Eliakim	2 Ch 12:13	
Lk 3:30	Jonan	1 Ki 14:31;	Abijah
Lk 3:30	Joseph	2 Ch 11:20; 13:21	
Lk 3:30	Juda	1 Ki 15:8-24	Asa
Lk 3:30	Simeon	2 Ch 15:17; 16:12	
Lk 3:29	Levi	1 Ki 15:24; 22:41-50	Jehoshaphat
Lk 3:29	Matthat	2 Ch 20:35-37	
Lk 3:29	Jorim	1 Ki 22:50; 2 Ki 8:16	Jehoram
Lk 3:29	Eliezer	2 Ch 21:14-20	
Lk 3:29	Jose	2 Ki 8:24-29; 9:16;	Ahaziah
Lk 3:28	Er	10:13; 2 Ch 22:9	
Lk 3:28	Elmodam	2 Ki 11:21; 12:1; 13:1	Joash
Lk 3:28	Cosam	2 Ki 12:21; 14:13	Amaziah
Lk 3:28	Addi	2 Ki 14:21; 15:1-27	Uzziah
Lk 3:28	Melchi	2 Ki 15:5, 30	Jotham
Lk 3:27	Neri	2 Ch 3:12; Is 7:1	
Lk 3:27	Salathiel	2 Ki 15:38; Is 7:1	Ahaz
Lk 3:27	Zerubbabel	2 Ki 18:1, 5:7	Hezekiah
Lk 3:27	Rhesa	1 Ch 3:13; Is 37:1	
Lk 3:27	Joanna	2 Ki 21:1; 1 Ch 3:132	Manasseh
Lk 3:26	Juda	2 Ki 21:19; 1 Ch 3:13	Amon
Lk 3:26	Joseph	1 Ki 13:2; 2 Ki 21:24	Josiah
Lk 3:26	Semei	2 Ki 23:34; 24:1-7	Jehoiakim
Lk 3:26	Mattathias	Jer 1:3, 25; 2 Ch 36:4	
Lk 3:26	Maath	2 Ki 24:6; 25:7	Jehoiachin
Lk 3:25	Nagge	2 Ch 36:4; Jer 22:24	
Lk 3:25	Esli	1 Ch 3:17, 19	Salathiel
Lk 3:25	Naum	Ez 3:2, 8; Ne 12:1	Zerubbabel
Lk 3:25	Amos	Ha 1:1, 12;,14; 2:2	
Lk 3:25	Mattathias	Mt 1:13	Abiud
Lk 3:24	Joseph	Mt 1:13	Eliakim
Lk 3:24	Janna	Mt 1:13	Azor
Lk 3:24	Melchi	Mt 1:14	Sadoc
Lk 3:24	Levi	Mt 1:14	Achim
Lk 3:24	Matthat	Mt 1:14	Eliud
Lk 3:23	Heli	Mt 1:15	Eleazar
		Mt 1:15	Matthan
		Mt 1:16	Jacob
	Joseph (Son-in-Law)		Joseph (husband of Mary)
	Mary [Luke 3]		**Joseph** [Matthew 1]

> **Solomon** - David's second son with Bathsheba. Their first died after David's sins of murder and adultery [2 Sam 11]. Overall, Solomon was a wise, good king (built the Temple)... yet he had problems later.

> **Rehoboam** - Solomon's son and heir to the throne became ruler of only 2 of the tribes of Israel (in Judah). As prophesied in Solomon's reign, the northern tribes broke away under separate leadership.

> **Hezekiah** - A good king that "reopened the doors of the Temple." He also built a tunnel to provide drinking water to the city of Jerusalem. It can be seen today. Inscriptions date it to the time of Hezekiah's reign.

> **Manasseh** - After becoming king at age 12, he was an evil king who built places of idol worship demolished by his predecessor, Hezekiah. He later repented.

> **Jeholachin** - Evil - He was cursed by God and told his family line would never inherit the throne of David... a seeming contradiction to prophecy about the line of Jesus [Jer 22:24-30].
>
> Since the genetic line of David went through Mary, and only the *legal* line through David, both the curse, and the promise of Jesus (as king) remained intact.

The Journey to Bethlehem

A hundred mile journey is taken for granted today... It's not even a plane ride. But imagine it thousands of years ago with no car, and over rugged terrain. It has a very different meaning.

For starters, consider walking. Suddenly it's a major trek. Next add steep hills and valleys. Difficulty increases. Finally, consider a pregnant, near-term wife with no doctors. A casual journey has become a major undertaking with considerable risk.

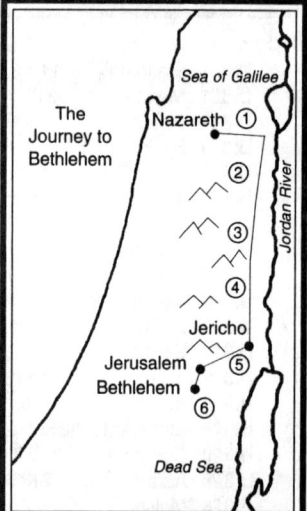

Joseph and Mary had to journey from Nazareth (population: about 200 families) to Bethlehem, Ephrathah to register for a census. (There was another Bethlehem near Nazareth.) It would take about 6 days [Lk 2:1-5].

Day one would have been a journey east towards the southern end of the Sea of Galilee. While a small amount of time might have been saved by going directly south through Samaria, it was common to avoid the land (Samarians were disdained by the Jews).

The next day a 60 mile trek down the river Jordan would begin. At least two nights would have to be spent in route before traveling into Jericho.

On day four or five, a rugged journey over the Judean wilderness would be made. In such a land filled with mountain lions, vipers, scorpions and bandits, Joseph and Mary would also face very treacherous terrain. It would have been an exhausting ordeal.

Finally Jerusalem, the highlight of the Journey would be reached. Presumably, Joseph and Mary would at least visit the Temple. After ceremonial washing, they would offer sacrifice of two Turtle Doves prior to heading southeast to Bethlehem.

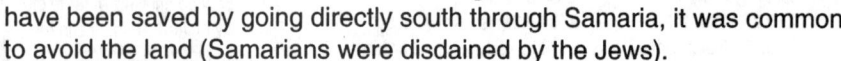

The trip from Jerusalem was short (two miles). Because of the required census, it would be bustling with out-of-towners, the reason why there would be no room at the inns of the area. That night, after an exhausting journey, with no hospital, no doctors - only the smell and noise of a stable - the God of the Universe would come to earth in a *completely dependent human form*... What an incredible and humble way to arrive.

The Night of Jesus' Birth

It probably started as a very ordinary night for the people of Bethlehem. After the fact we can see extraordinary events taking place and even wonder why there wasn't room at the inn, or why there were no crowds.

To keep things in perspective, we need to understand the world at that time. There was no CNN late night news. There were no newspapers... not even much writing at all. No phones. Travel was very limited. Joseph and Mary -100 miles from home - might as well have been thousands of miles away. There was no communication whatsoever.

In a short 9 months under incredible duress from a unique pregnancy, it would have been unusual for Mary's family to broadcast her condition to other cities. Presumably, they kept it quiet (Joseph had even planned to "quietly divorce" Mary until an angel intervened - Mt 1:19).

The Inn and Stable

The inn mentioned in the *Bible* (Greek - *kataluma*) could have been a major structure, a house or simply a shelter. The caravauserai, or Eastern inns common at the time were large buildings (about 100 yards on each side) formed around a large central courtyard where animals were kept. In such a case Jesus would have been born in the central courtyard on a ledge that served as the feeding area (or manger). More likely he was born in a cave (commonly used as a stable)... such as the site celebrated as the birthplace of Jesus in Bethlehem today [p 11].

The Angels

One of the purposes of angels was foretelling great news, as did Gabriel regarding the births of John the Baptist [Luke 1:19] and Jesus [Luke 1:26]. The only other mention of Gabriel is in Daniel, to prophesy Jesus' entry into Jerusalem to become the ultimate sacrifice for Mankind [see page 12-13]. Hence, Gabriel foretold both the birth of the Savior and the rebirth of Mankind.

Songs of angels often seem synonymous with Christmas. However, only <u>twice</u> does the *Bible* mention angels singing: Once at creation, before the fall of Man [Job 38:7] and once at the end times [Rev 5:8-10], after Adam's curse is removed.

A Solitary Birth

It was common in Jesus' time to utilize midwives in childbirth. Almost never was a birth undertaken alone, and it would have been unusual to have a pregnant woman rejected at the inn. Yet the Biblical account seems to indicate that Mary was virtually on her own at the birth (Luke 2:7 states "she" wrapped the baby in swaddling cloths and placed him in a manger... things typically done by a midwife). Mary was only a teenager or woman in her early twenties at the time.

The Magi

The account of the visit of the Magi at first seems simply a colorful story emphasizing the "mystery" of the birth of Jesus. In reality, the Magi were a very important part of the politics of the region at the time.

During the years preceding the birth of Jesus, there were numerous struggles between Rome and Persia. Palestine was essentially a "buffer state." Herod was granted the title "King of the Jews" three full years before he was able to occupy his own capital city (he was previously driven out by the Persians). Hence, Herod (a half Jew) was extremely insecure in his role. Furthermore, "full" Jews looked down on Herod. So the potential existed for Herod to be attacked from many directions including potential collusion between the Jews and Persians.

Add to this the fact that the ruler of Persia was aging and in ill-health. The Magi were given great power and often played key roles in the governmental affairs. Duties included selecting the kings of Persia. Hence, an environment was in place that would certainly have "greatly troubled" the insecure Herod and the people of Jerusalem [Mt 2:3]. In summary, we have:

- An insecure king (Herod - killed even his own family)
- A history of conflict with Persia
- A volatile situation with the ruler of Persia (old and ill)
- With powerful "kingmakers" (Magi) visiting Herod
- Seeking the "King of the Jews" (a title Herod held)

It's no surprise the Magi got an audience with Herod (who was concerned that disputes could launch a new major conflict). The Magi arrived with great "pomp" and ceremony. Despite the myths of three "kings" on camels, Magi would have rode in on horses, complete with their own army. And the Magi were not "kings." Herod even tolerated the obvious insult... seeking a baby "King of the Jews" (Herod had that title). Not unlike today, Herod honored their presence, then proceded with his own plan - killing all male babies in the area that might be a threat.

How the Magi Knew

How did the Magi know to come to Palestine, at that time, in search of the new king? The answer is the prophet Daniel... appointed chief over the Magi during Exile [Dan 5:11]. Daniel was given the precise prophecy of when the Messiah would enter Jerusalem as King [pp 12-13]. Other prophecy of a sign (star) to indicate the coming Messiah would also be known by them. For whatever reason, the prophecy about Bethlehem (*Micah* 5:2) was not yet fully recognized by the Magi.

When Was Jesus Born?

The most widely referenced date of all time is the date of Jesus' birth. Yet, it's probably wrong. A monk named Dionysius Exiguus estimated the year of Jesus' birth in 532 AD. Today, our calendar uses that estimate as a reference for any year BC (Before Christ) or AD. Evidence suggests that Exiguus mis-estimated by as many as one to seven years.

4 BC ?

The most commonly assumed (real) date of Jesus' birth is 4 BC. The basis for this year, is a reference by the Jewish historian Josephus, of an eclipse "shortly before" Herod the Great's death. (The presumed eclipse occurred on March 13, 4 BC[12] - although another eclipse occurred in 1 BC). Herod was alive at the time of Jesus birth [Mt 2]. Using that information, 4 BC would be the closest possible year to the original estimate. Many Biblical resources suggest this date.

7 BC ?

A date of 7 BC for the star of Bethlehem was proposed by observations of Kepler (yet several alternative possibilities exist) . Kepler's timing is supported by information about historical Roman censuses (which would have occurred about 7-8 BC). However some scholars suggest other censuses occurred as well, and argue there is no firm evidence which census, and what local timing, actually brought Joseph and Mary to Bethlehem. Since alternatives exist for both the star and the census, there is no certainty that 7 BC is correct.

2 BC ?

The most exhaustive evidence may support a date of 2 BC[12]. Several approaches seem to corroborate the date:

1. Both the *Magillath Ta'anith* (an ancient Jewish scroll contemporary with Jesus) and *Judaeos* (c. 8 AD) indicate Herod died on January 14, 1 BC.

2. Tertullian (160 AD) indicated that Augustus died 15 years after the birth of Jesus (and began ruling 41 years prior to the birth). The historical death of Augustus on August 19, 14 AD would place the birth of Jesus in 2 BC.*

3. Irenaeus indicated Jesus was born in the 41st year of August (see above).

4. "Father of Church History" Eusebius (265-340 AD) seemed to agree with the Augustus references above and also tied the birth of Jesus to the deaths of Anthony and Cleopatra further confirming 2 BC.

5. Working backwards from the beginning of the ministry of Jesus and John the Baptist an estimate of 2 BC would seem most likely. We know the ministries began in the 15 year of the reign of Tiberius Caesar, which history pinpoints as 29 AD [Lk 3:1]. Jewish law required men to be 30 before starting ministry and Luke indicates Jesus was "about 30 years old" [Lk 3:23]. Working backwards would place the birth in 2 BC.

*Note: There is no year zero, which must be taken into account in calculations.

Was Jesus Just a Man?

Accepting the eyewitness testimony may still leave questions for some. The manuscripts didn't merely indicate that a great man named Jesus was born. They indicate God came to earth in human flesh. That Jesus was born of a virgin... created by God's Holy Spirit. They indicate Jesus performed miracles helping prove he was the Son of God. And that he became the Savior of the world when he rose from the dead after a violent crucifixion. How do we know Jesus was not just a "good teacher" or "prophet"? Some compelling reasons are:

1. Those *KNOWING THE TRUTH* died violent deaths to prove it.[8]

People who were with Jesus constantly during his ministry, the disciples, knew for a fact whether Jesus had proven himself God by overcoming death. All but John, died a violent death rather than renounce the gospel.

Peter- Crucified upside down	Bartholomew- Crucified
James (Jesus' brother)- Stoned	Andrew- Crucified
Matthew- Death by sword	Philip- Crucified
James (Alphaeus)- Crucified	Simon- Crucified
James (Zebedee)- Death by sword	Thomas- Speared
Thaddaeus - Killed by Arrows	Paul- Beheaded
John- Natural Death	

Martyrdom for a cause is not unusual. But martyrdom for a lie - *when the truth is known* - makes no sense. The disciples knew of Jesus' claim to be God. They knew of his promise to overcome death. They saw him die. They were in a position to KNOW for certain if his resurrection was real. Why would anyone - let alone 12 people - die for a God that was a fake?

2. Millions chose death over renouncing Jesus. Underneath Rome lie 900 miles of carved caves - the "Catacombs" - where over seven million Christians were buried. Many of these graves are of people who chose vicious execution, rather than renounce Jesus. Early Christians hiding in the Catacombs inevitably spoke directly with eyewitnesses of Jesus. Since about 400 AD. the Catacombs were buried and "forgotten" for over 1000 years. In 1578 they were rediscovered by accident. Today they can be seen as silent memorials to many who died rather than curse Jesus or bow down to an emperor's statue.

Was Jesus Just a "Great Prophet"?

Some non-Believing Jews and others say that Jesus was a "great prophet," but not the Messiah and not the son of God.

Such a statement is self-contradictory. A prophet by definition had to be 100% accurate. Jesus gave prophecy indicating that he was both the Messiah and the son of God. So if Jesus was a great prophet, he also had to be the Messiah and the son of God. Otherwise, he was not a prophet.

Considering Jesus' track record on other easily verified prophecies, we would be wise to also believe his more significant claims [see p 26].

3. <u>Paul, one of the greatest persecutors of Christians, changed radically upon seeing the risen Christ</u>. Hostile testimony from people representing an opposing viewpoint, is often the most compelling. Paul, *a leader of the effort to execute Christians*, gave up wealth, prestige and power to spread the gospel after encountering the risen Christ. Paul went from being a prominent Pharisee to being poverty-stricken, tortured, stoned, shipwrecked, and eventually beheaded [Acts 22, 2 Cor 11:22-23]. His efforts resulted in much of the *New Testament* and the start of many early Christian churches.

4. <u>Prophecies written hundreds of years before Jesus identify him specifically</u>. Prophecies with details regarding the "Who? What? When? Where", of Jesus, were recorded centuries before the First Christmas. We have, in existence today, ancient manuscripts of hundreds of precise prophecies [pp 12-13].

How Do We Know Records are Accurate?

Scribes

Being a Jewish scribe was considered one of the most demanding and esteemed positions in *Biblical* times. Scribes were trained for years and were permitted to practice the profession only after age thirty. They were sometimes referred to as Doctors of the Law, and joined the priests in helping others understand the Law.

Scriptural Copy Rules

Recording of Holy Scripture was a serious responsibility. So important was the exact reproduction, that scribes were forced to adhere to demanding rules any time a manuscript was copied:

1. Scrolls - special paper, ink and surface preparation.
2. Tight specifications - column number, 37 letters per column.
3. Master used - no duplicates of duplicates.
4. Each letter - visually confirmed. No writing of phrases.
5. Distance between letters - checked with thread.
6. Alphabet - each letter counted and compared to original.
7. Letters per page - counted and compared to master.
8. Middle letter of scroll - verified to be same as master.
9. ONE MISTAKE - scroll was destroyed.

The Dead Sea Scrolls

Any doubt regarding the accurate transmission of manuscripts was erased in 1947 with the discovery of hundreds of scrolls buried for nearly 2,000 years. Many were written over 100 years BC. Comparison with recent Jewish copies show virtually no change.

Was Jesus God?

Christians claim that Jesus was in reality God appearing to the world in human flesh. The Christian concept of the one God of the universe includes three distinctly different, yet inextricable parts: The Father, the Son (Jesus) and the Holy Spirit. Though somewhat difficult to understand, analogies have been made to H_2O which can exist as water, ice and gas... or to light, having quantum, wave and physical properties.

Did Jesus Think He Was God?

Many times Jesus referred to his own Deity, both directly and indirectly. Although Jesus confirmed that he was the Messiah [Mk 14:62-63] he did not use the term "Messiah" to refer to himself - perhaps to differentiate his Deity from the widespread *expectation of a human Messiah*. Jesus used the terms Son of Man and Son of God often. Both referred to his Divine nature [Dan 7:13-14, Mt 26:63-64]. Jesus also used the specific words "I am" (*Ego eimi* in Greek, *Ani bu* in Hebrew) on several occasions (e.g. John 8:56-58). God used these same words to describe himself to Moses. Jesus also states specifically that he and God are "One" [John 10:30].

Jesus clearly indicated he had authority over issues controlled only by God, such as forgiveness of sin [Mk 2:5-10], the timeless power of his words [Mt 24:35] and glory [John 17:5]. Also significant, was Jesus' acceptance of worship [Lk 5:8, John 20:28]. The intense monotheistic foundation of the Jews would absolutely forbid any worship of anything but the one true God. Analysis of Jesus' life... his compassionate miracles, his perfect life-style, and his love... support his claims... providing additional evidence of Divinity.

Did Others Think He Was God?

The disciples came to view Jesus as God in human flesh and worshiped him as such [Lk 5:8, John 20:28]. Witnessing of the Resurrection and the Transfiguration [Mt 17:1] provided strong evidence. Early Christian writing defines Jesus to be God... *our Lord*... here on earth [1 Cor 8:6, 1 Tim 2:5].

Is There Other Evidence?

Many say Jesus' miracles are evidence of Deity. But miracles have been recorded as being performed by others (in the *Bible* and elsewhere). The *Bible* states that perfect fulfillment of prophecy proves God's intervention [Deut 18:21-22]. The odds of all *Old Testament* prophecies about Jesus, coming true in **any** one man is beyond statistical possibility without Divine intervention (pp. 12-13). Jesus prophesied with perfect accuracy regarding such things as the precise timing of his death, the detailed manner of his death, his resurrection and his later appearance in Galilee. Prophetic perfection combined with a claim to be God verifies Jesus' Deity.

Common Questions

The Star

Many Planetariums acknowledge the conjunction of Jupiter, Saturn in the constellation of "The Fishes" in 7 BC. Clay tablets found in Babylonia *written the year before*, indicate the Magi were looking forward to the event as one of great significance. Symbolically, Jupiter represented a world ruler. Saturn was regarded the "star" of Palestine and "The Fishes" represented the "last days". This knowledge combined with the *Biblical* prophecies, which Daniel inevitably taught the Magi, may have initiated the Magi journey to see Jesus. Even other prophecy not contained in the *Bible* may have started this journey. However, there are many other possible explanations of the "star of Bethlehem" including that of a "nova" (a star that increases in brightness).

The final guidance to the location of Jesus [Mt 2:9] was more likely a different manifestation of God's glory, sometimes referred to as "shekinah" glory. Other examples of shekinah glory in the *Bible* are the cloud of the exodus [Exodus 13:21], and the glory that shone on the shepherds [Luke 2:9]

Gifts of the Magi

Gold, Frankincense and Myrrh were significant gifts considering the role of Jesus for the world. Gold, the most precious metal at the time, was the symbol for royalty. Frankincense was an expensive fragrance which played a special role in worship (Lev 2:2). And Myrrh was an embalming substance (a surprising gift for a newborn baby). Together they describe Jesus as a Savior for the world (Myrrh - for the blood sacrifice), that would receive ultimate ruling authority (Gold - Kingship) and worship (Incense).

The Date of Christmas

The First Christmas probably occurred in the spring or summer - a more likely time for shepherds to be in the fields (almost never after October). The pagan holiday, Saturnalia, traditionally began on December 19 and was characterized by feasting, gift giving, special music, lighting of candles, green trees and great revelry. As Christianity spread, this holiday was given Christian connotations. The official Roman holiday of Christmas was decreed by Emperor Constantine in 336 AD. However, because of the pagan origin, Christmas was actually outlawed in England in the 1600's and banned in some areas until recently.

Why Do Some Reject Jesus?

With the wealth of evidence, it seems incredible that some (including many Jews) reject Jesus as the Messiah. This, however, was clearly prophesied [Is 53:1-3, Ps 118:22, Mt 21:42-46, Luke 16:19-31]. We also need to realize that many do accept Jesus as the Messiah (including Jews). Virtually all of the "first Christians" were Jews and Christianity wasn't officially separated from Judaism until it began to threaten the early Jewish leaders. Some scholars estimate that about 70% of Jerusalem was Christian when conquered in 70 AD.

Common Questions

What if I Don't Believe the Entire *Bible*?

Having a relationship with God does not depend on believing the entire *Bible*. Belief in Jesus as Savior, and asking him to be director of your life is all that is required. Some people wonder why God uses prophecy and sometimes "cryptic" wording. There is no absolute answer to this. Perhaps God wants people to seek him and then find him? Perhaps he wants to emphasize faith? Or perhaps he wants to allow the Holy Spirit to reach people differently? Even so, general evidence is also abundant.

How Can We Ensure the Right Relationship to Go to Heaven?

When Jesus said not all who use his name will enter heaven [Mt 7:21-23] he was referring to people who think using Christ's name along with rituals and rules is the key to heaven. A *relationship* with God is NOT based on rituals and rules. It's based on grace and forgiveness, and the right kind of relationship with him.

How to Have a Personal Relationship with God

1. **B**elieve that God exists and that he came to earth in the human form of Jesus Christ. [John 3:16; Rom 10:9]
2. **A**ccept God's free forgiveness of sins through the death and resurrection of Jesus Christ. [Eph 2:8-10; Eph 1:7-8]
3. **S**witch to God's plan for life. [1 Pet 1:21-23; Eph 2:1-5]
4. **E**xpress desire for Christ to be director of your life. [Mt 7:21-27; 1 John 4:15]

Prayer for Eternal Life with God

"Dear God, I believe you sent your son, Jesus, to die for my sins so I can be forgiven. I'm sorry for my sins and I want to live the rest of my life the way you want me to. Please put your Spirit in my life to direct me. Amen."

Then What?

People who have sincerely taken the above steps automatically become members of God's family of Believers. A new world of freedom and strength is available through prayer and obedience to God's will. New Believers can build their relationship with God with the following steps:

- ❑ Find a *Bible*-based church that you like, and attend regularly.
- ❑ Try to set aside some time each day to pray and read the *Bible*.
- ❑ Locate other Christians to spend time with on a regular basis.

God's Promises to Believers

For Today

But seek first his kingdom and his righteousness, and all these things *[e.g. things to satisfy all your needs]* will be given to you as well. Mt 6:33

For Eternity

Whoever believes in the Son has eternal life, but whoever rejects the Son will not see life, for God's wrath remains on him. John 3:36

Once we develop an eternal perspective, even the greatest problems on earth fade in significance.

References

1. *Encyclopedia Britannica*, Chicago, IL: 1993.
2. Free, Joseph P. and Vos, Howard F. *Archaeology and Bible History*, Grand Rapids, MI: Zondervan, 1969.
3. Freeman, James M., *Manners and Customs of the Bible*, Plainfield, NJ, LOGOS International, 1972.
4. Green, Michael, *Who is This Jesus?*, Nashville, Thomas Nelson, 1992.
5. Hirshberg & Simon; LIFE MAGAZINE; *The First Christmas;* New York, NY: Dec 1992.
6. Josephus, Flavius. Translated by Whiston, Wm., *The Complete Works of Josephus*, Grand Rapids, MI: Kregel, 1981.
7. Keely, Robin, *Jesus 2000*, Batavia, IL: Lion Publishing plc, 1989
8. MacArthur, John F. Jr., *God With Us*, Grand Rapids, MI, Zondervan Publishing House, 1989.
9. Mc Dowell, Josh and Wilson, Bill, *A Ready Defense*, San Bernadino, CA Here's Life Publishers, Inc., 1990.
10. Mc Dowell, Josh and Wilson, Bill, *He Walked Among Us*, Nashville, TN: Thomas Nelson, Inc., 1993.
11. McRay, John, Archaeology & the New Testament, Grand Rapids, MI: Baker Book House, 1991.
12. Missler, Chuck, *Christmas Story* Audio Tape, Coeur d'Alene, ID: Koinonia House Inc., 1995.
13. Missler, Chuck, *Footprints of the Messiah*, Audio Tape, Coeur d'Alene, ID: Koinonia House Inc., 1995.
14. Missler, Chuck, *Romance of Redemption*, Audio Tape, Coeur d'Alene, ID: Koinonia House Inc., 1995.
15. Muncaster, Ralph O., *The Bible - General Analysis - Investigation of the Evidence*, Mission Viejo, CA: Strong Basis to Believe, 1996.
16. Muncaster, Ralph O., *Jesus - Investigation of the Evidence*, Mission Viejo, CA: Strong Basis to Believe, 1996.
17. Readers Digest, *ABC's of the Bible*, Pleasantville, NY, 1991.
18. Readers Digest, *Who's Who in the Bible*, Pleasantville, NY, 1994.
19. Rosen, Moishe, *Y'shua*, Chicago, IL: Moody Bible Institute, 1982.
20. Ross, Hugh, Ph.D., *The Fingerprint of God*, Orange, CA: Promise Publishing Co., 1989.
21. Shanks, Hershel (editor), *Understanding the Dead Sea Scrolls*, New York, NY: Vintage Books, 1993.
22. Smith, F. LaGard, *The Daily Bible In Chronological Order*, Eugine, OR: Harvest House, 1984.
23. Walvoord, John F., *The Prophecy Knowledge Handbook*, Wheaton, IL: Victor Books, 1984.
24. Youngblood, Ronald F., *New Illustrated Bible Dictionary*, Nashville, TN: Nelson, 1995.

Investigation of the Evidence
by Ralph O. Muncaster

Jesus Christ Series

Jesus
    Evidence supporting the existence and role of Jesus Christ. History, archaeology and prophecy verifies reality of Jesus. Evidence supports Deity of Jesus and reviews his purpose.

First Easter
    Information about Jesus specific to the Resurrection, including analysis of historical dating and events.

First Christmas
    Information about Jesus specific to the First Christmas. Popular misconceptions of the Magi, angels, the star, the date of Jesus' birth and other items are clarified with the actual facts.

The Bible Series

Bible - General Analysis
    Facts regarding the development of the *Bible*. Analyzes manuscript evidence, archaeological support, prophecies, scientific accuracy and "hidden evidence". Confirms the reliability of the *Bible*.

Bible - Prophecy Miracles
    Summarizes many of the 100% accurate, precision prophecies written in the *Bible*... centuries in advance.

Bible - Hidden Evidence   [Coming Soon]
    Incredible hidden evidence that statistically "proves" Divine planning.

Bible - Scientific Insights
    Biblical scientific insights that were correct long before science was.

Bible - Archaeological Facts   [Coming Soon]
    Discoveries that demonstrate Biblical accuracy... even when scholars were wrong.

Bible - Manuscript Reliability   [Coming Soon]
    The amazing manuscript evidence: development, survival and history.

Other

Creation   [Coming Soon]
    Analyzes the *Biblical* account of Creation relative to modern science, molecular biology and statistical analysis. Compares likelihood of Creation to probability of Evolution. Reviews the fossil record and describes proven hoaxes of anthropology... sometimes left uncorrected in books and articles, even today.